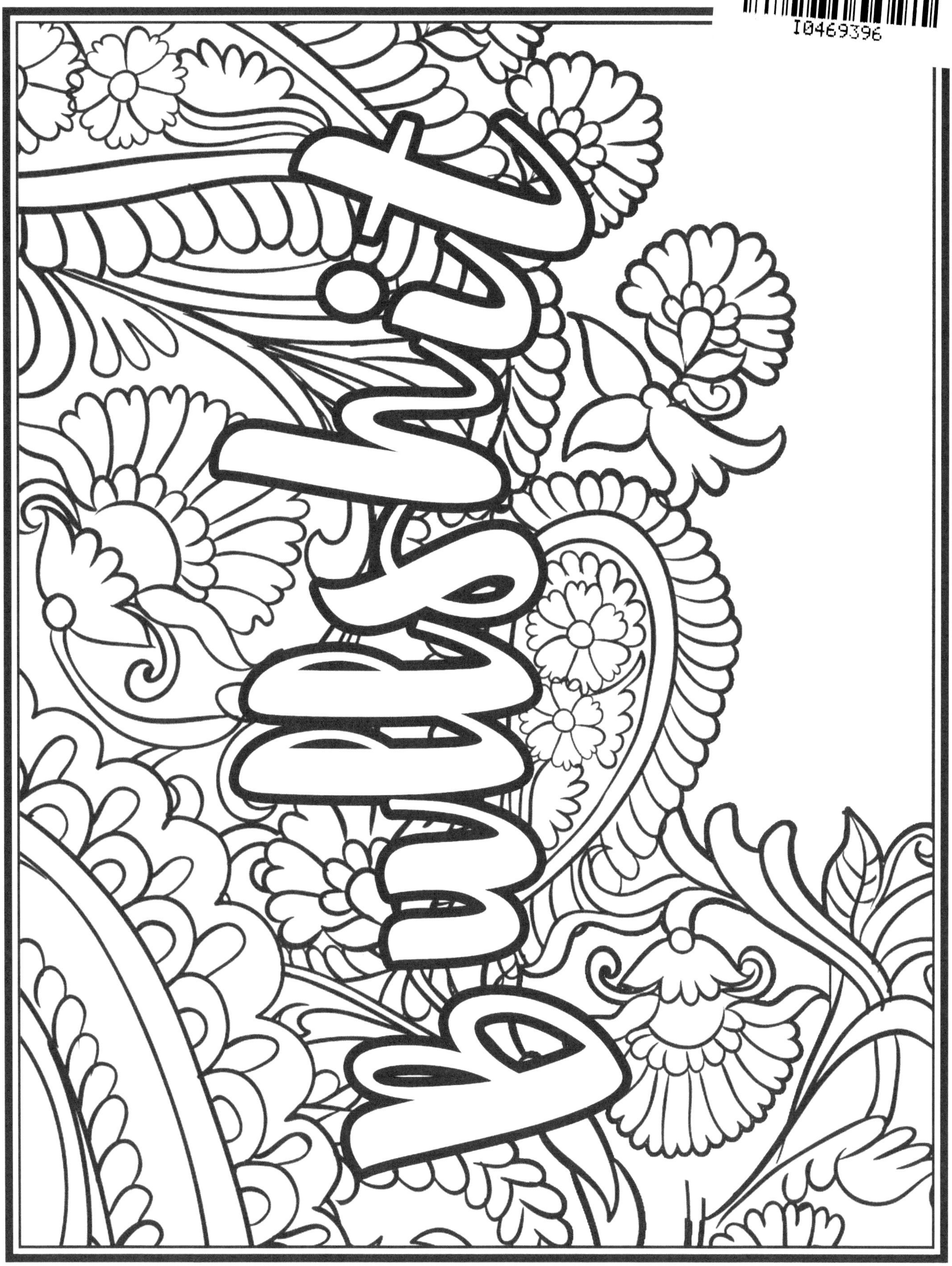
be happy

By Artists:
Joshua Lazana Lagman and Jade Villaremo
Mandala & Caricature Illustration
Art Director: lluontheloose

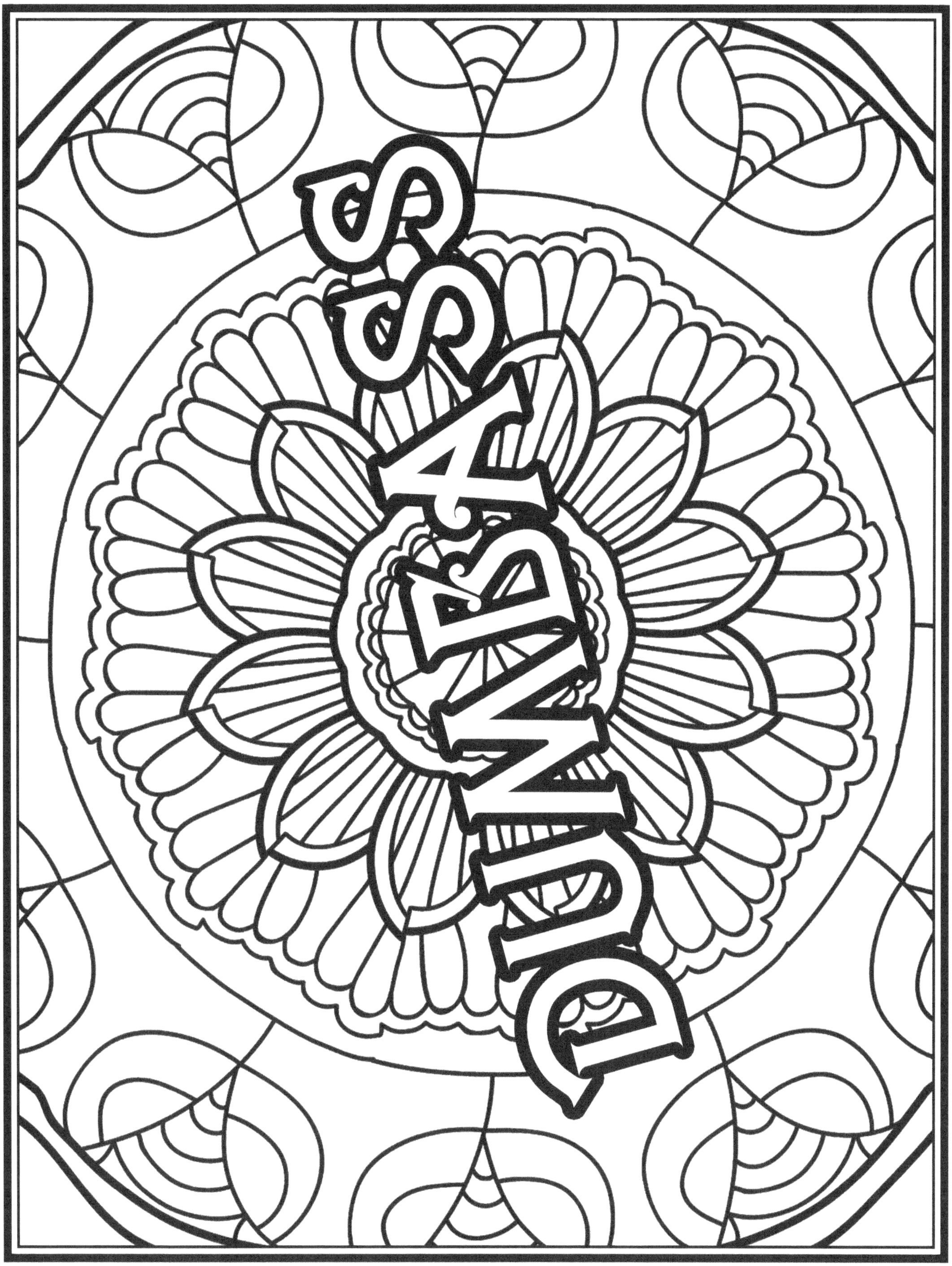
DUMBASS

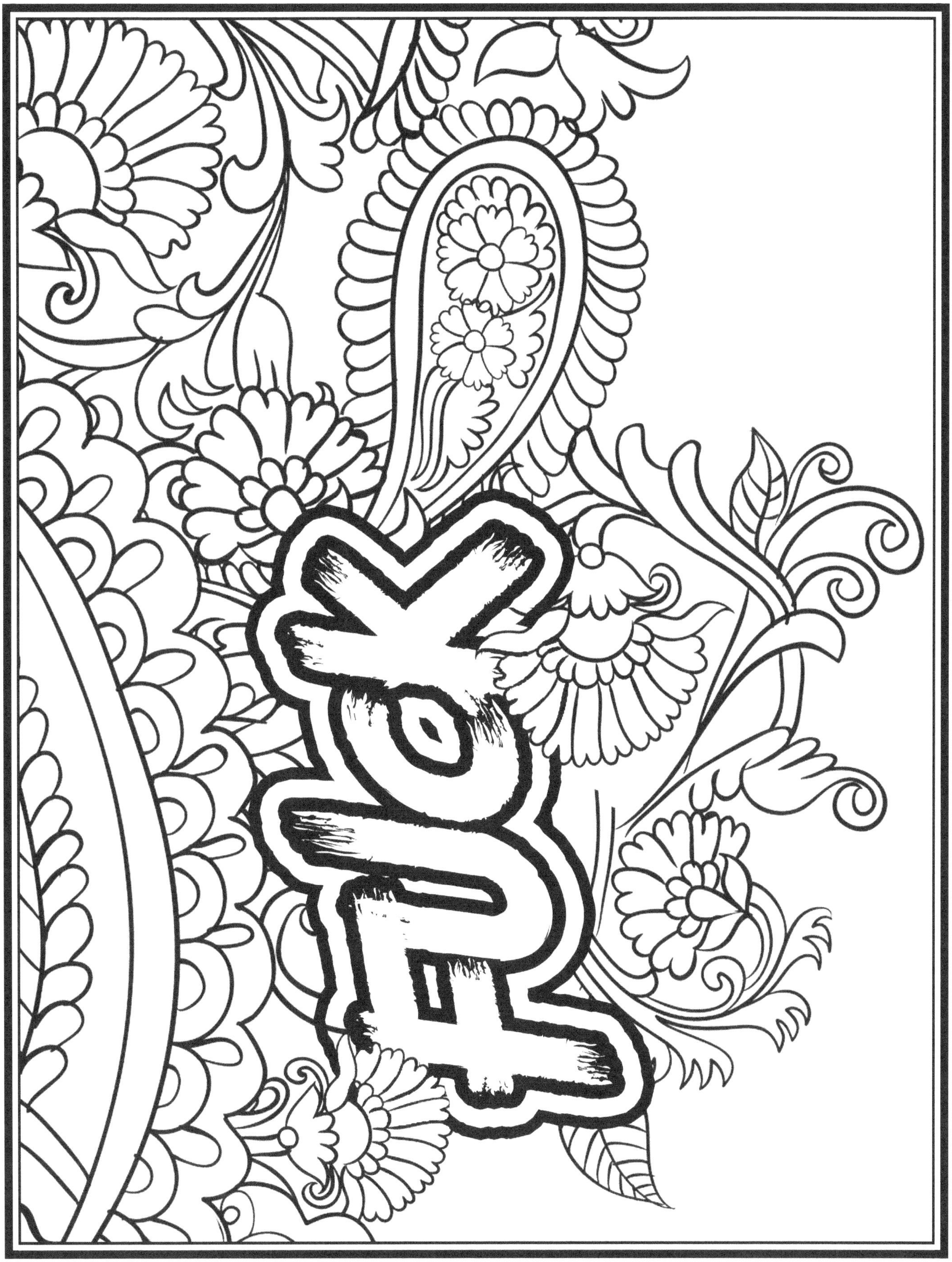
Fuck

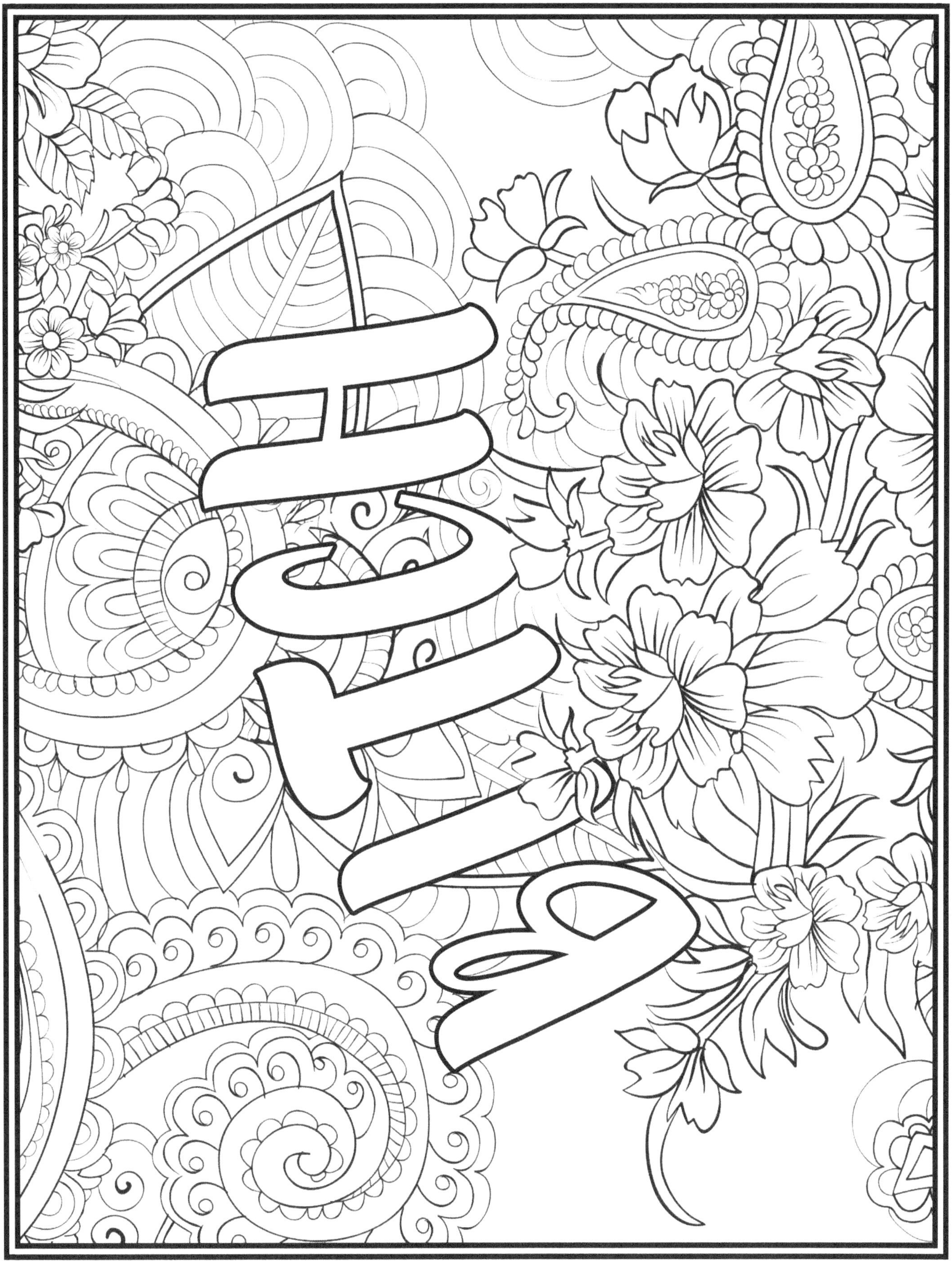
BITCH

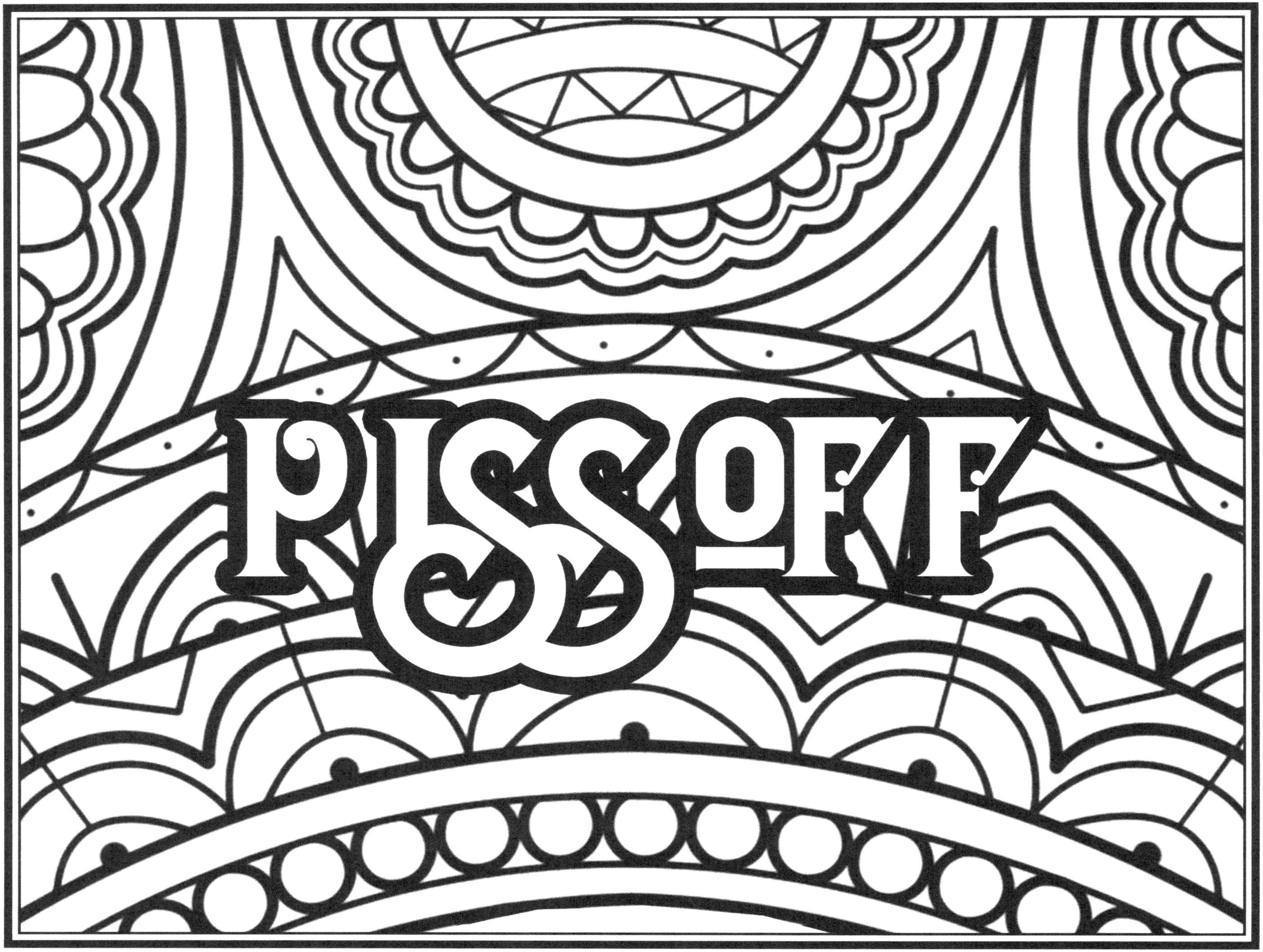
PISS OFF

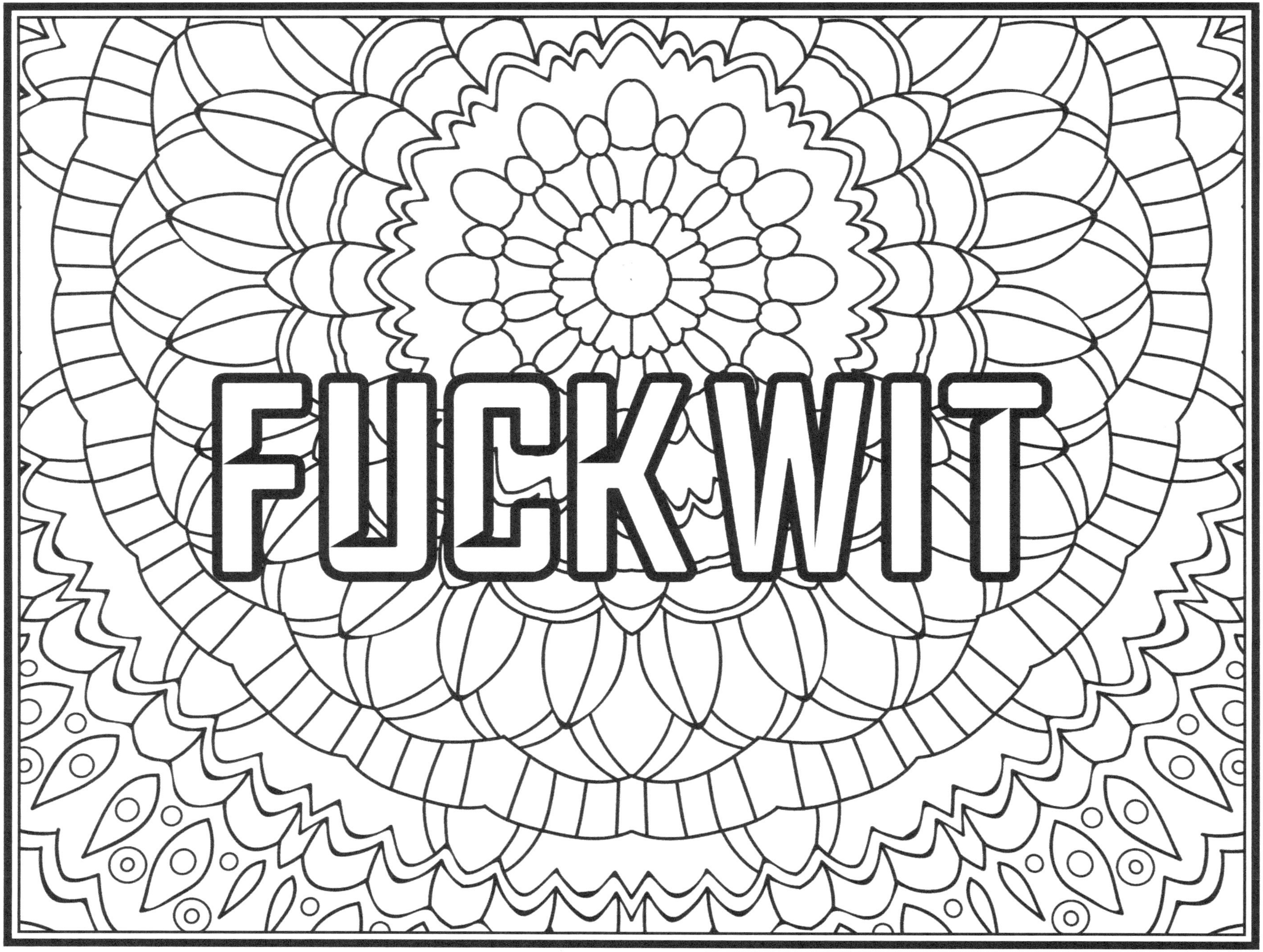
FUCKWIT

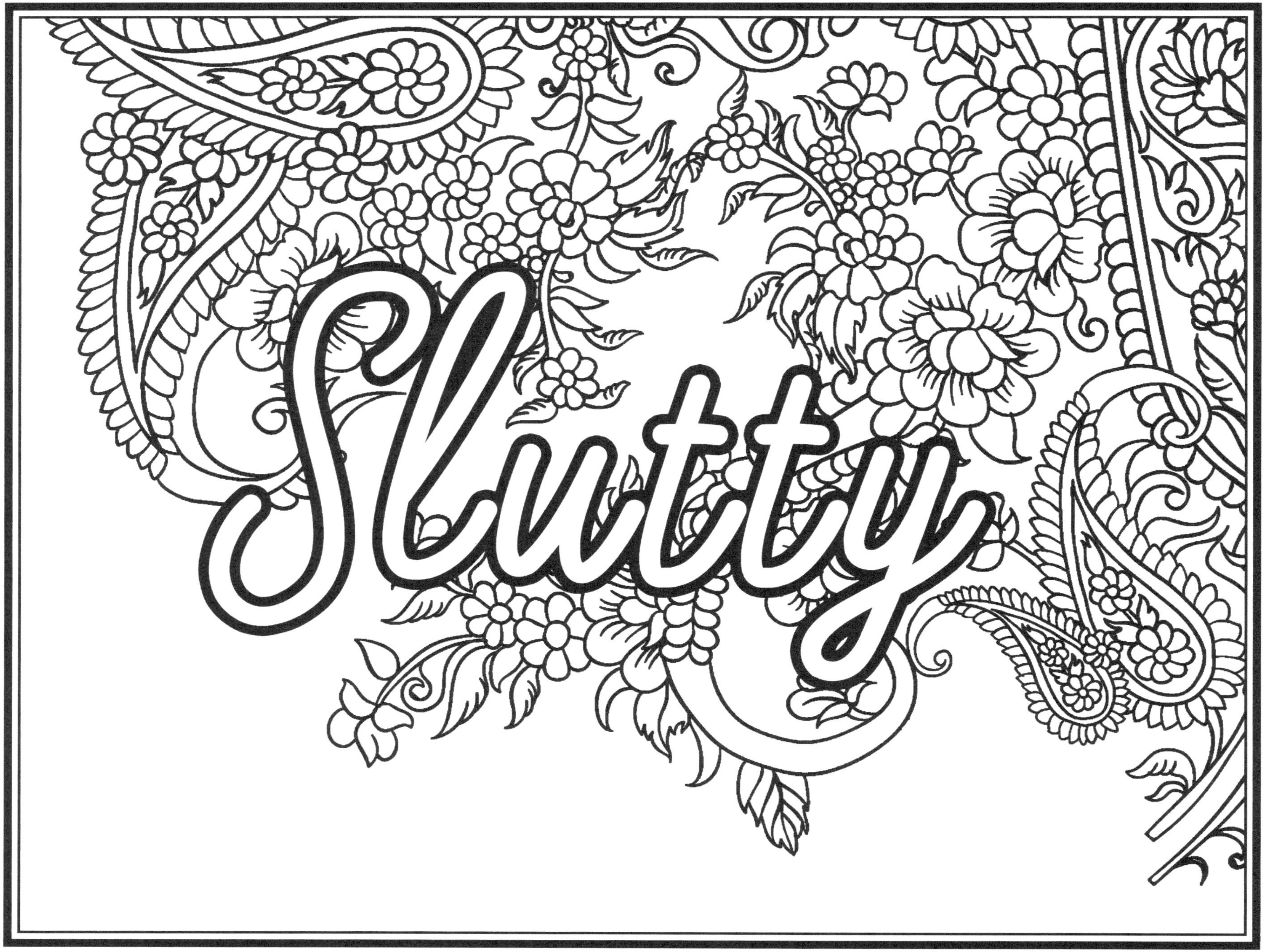
Slutty

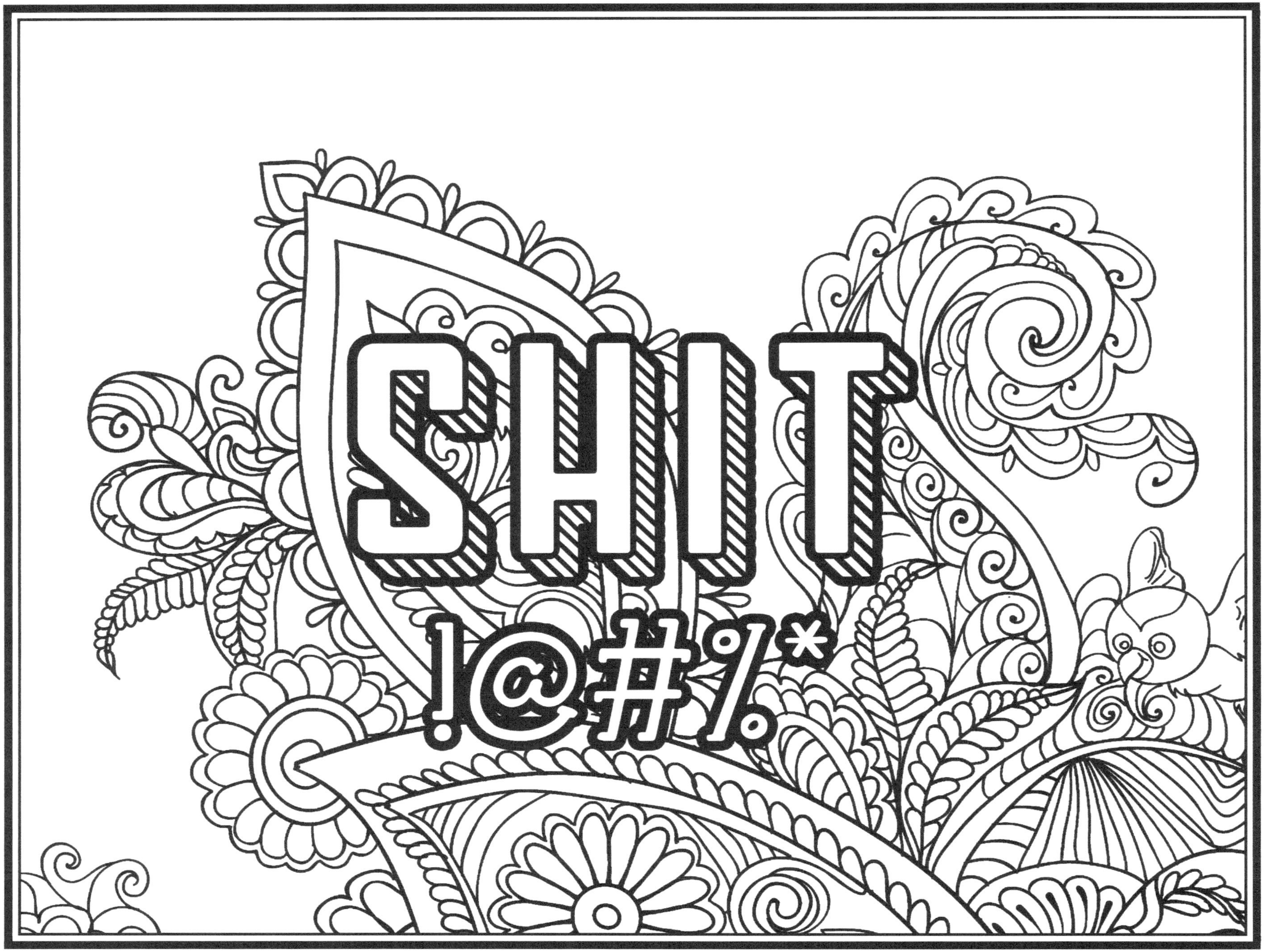
SHIT
!@#%*

WHORE

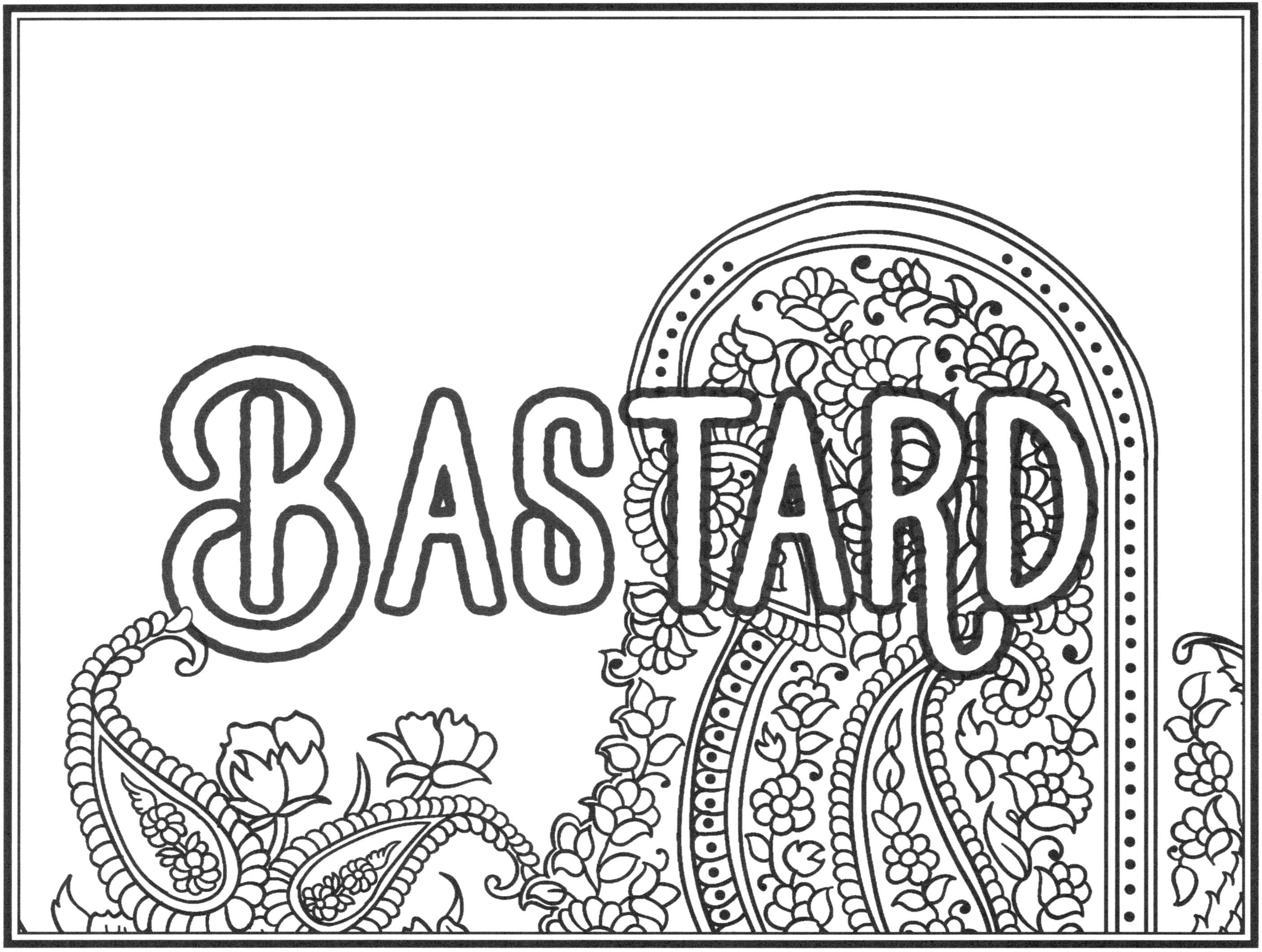
BASTARD

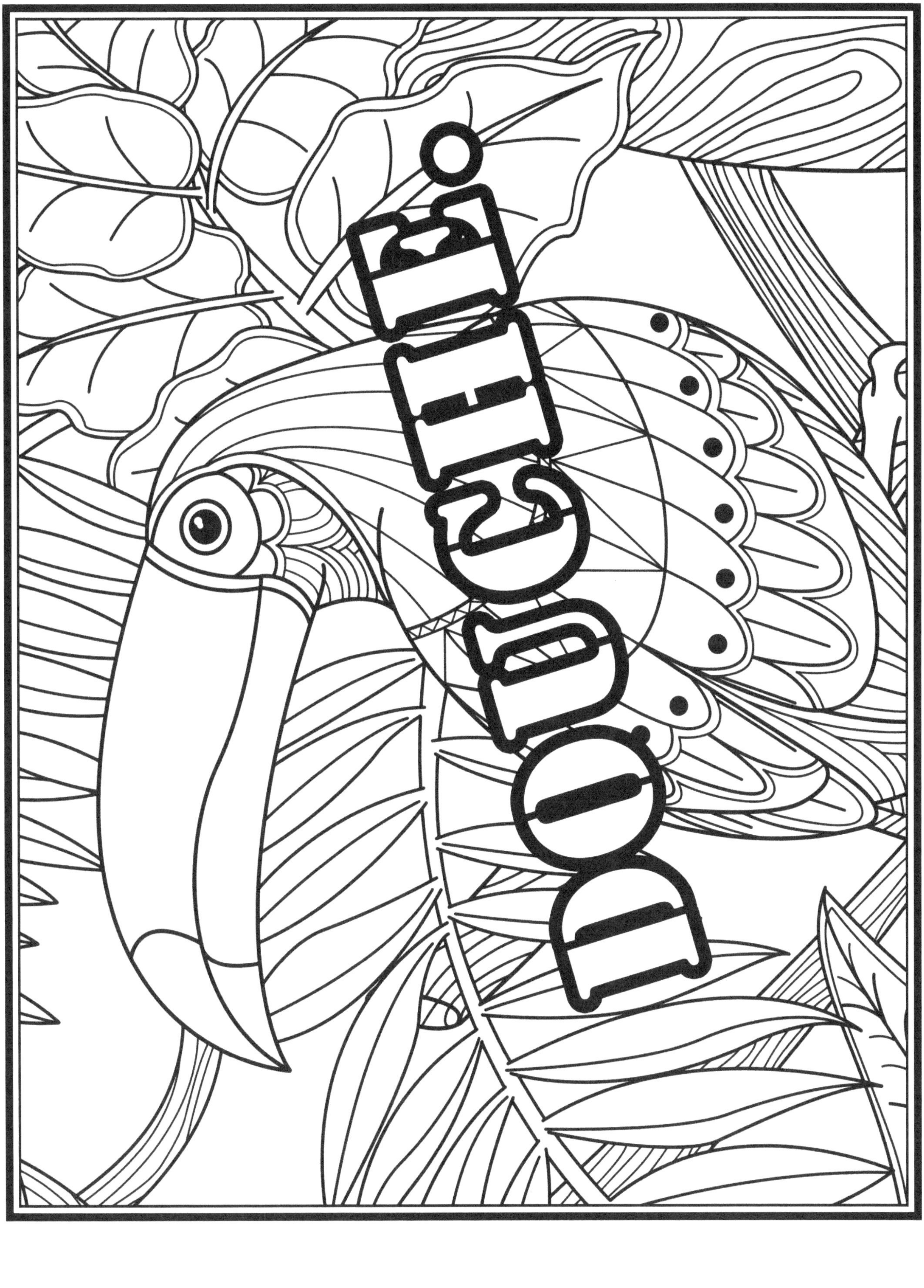
DOUCHE!

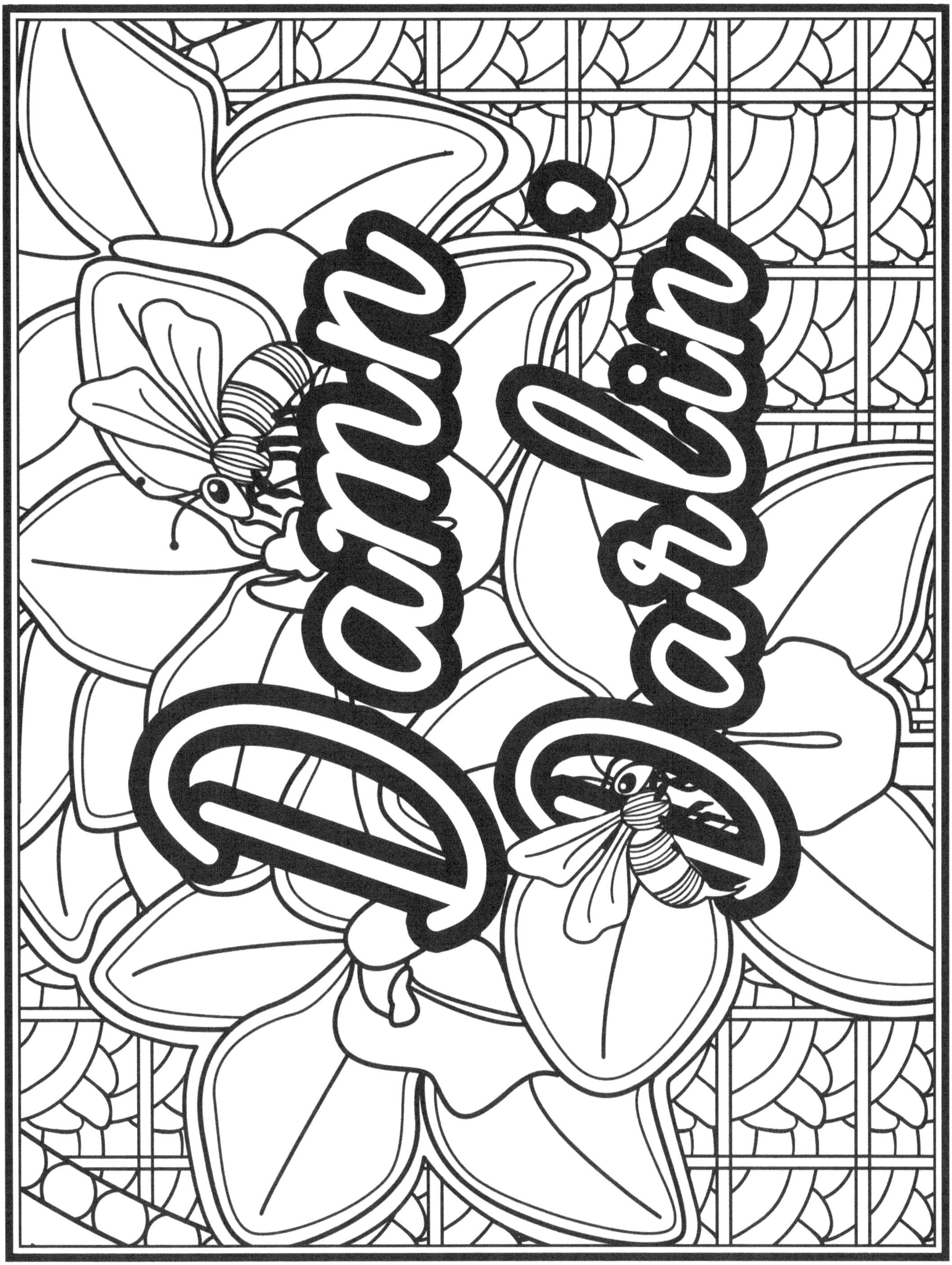
Damn Darlin'

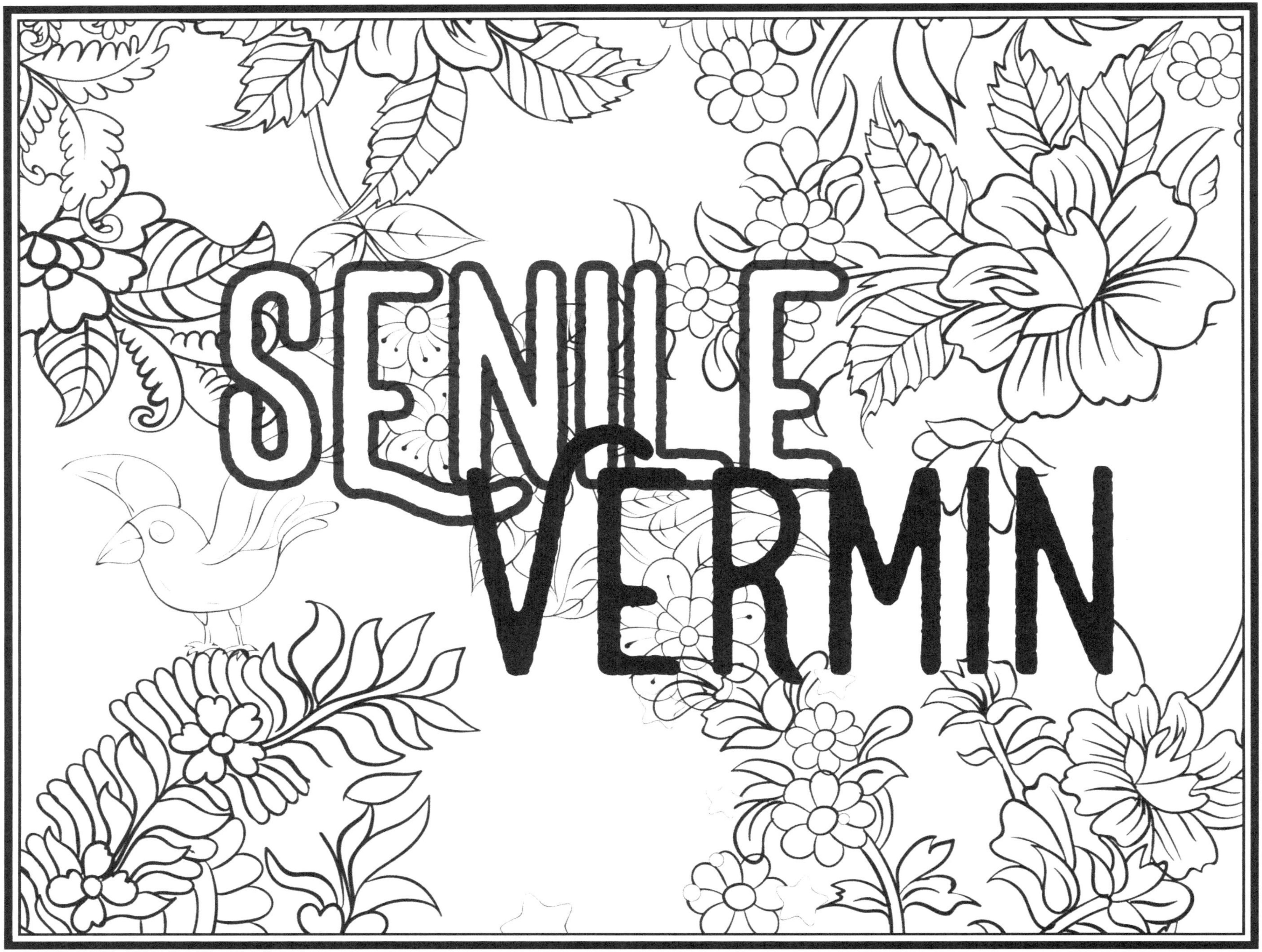
SENILE
VERMIN

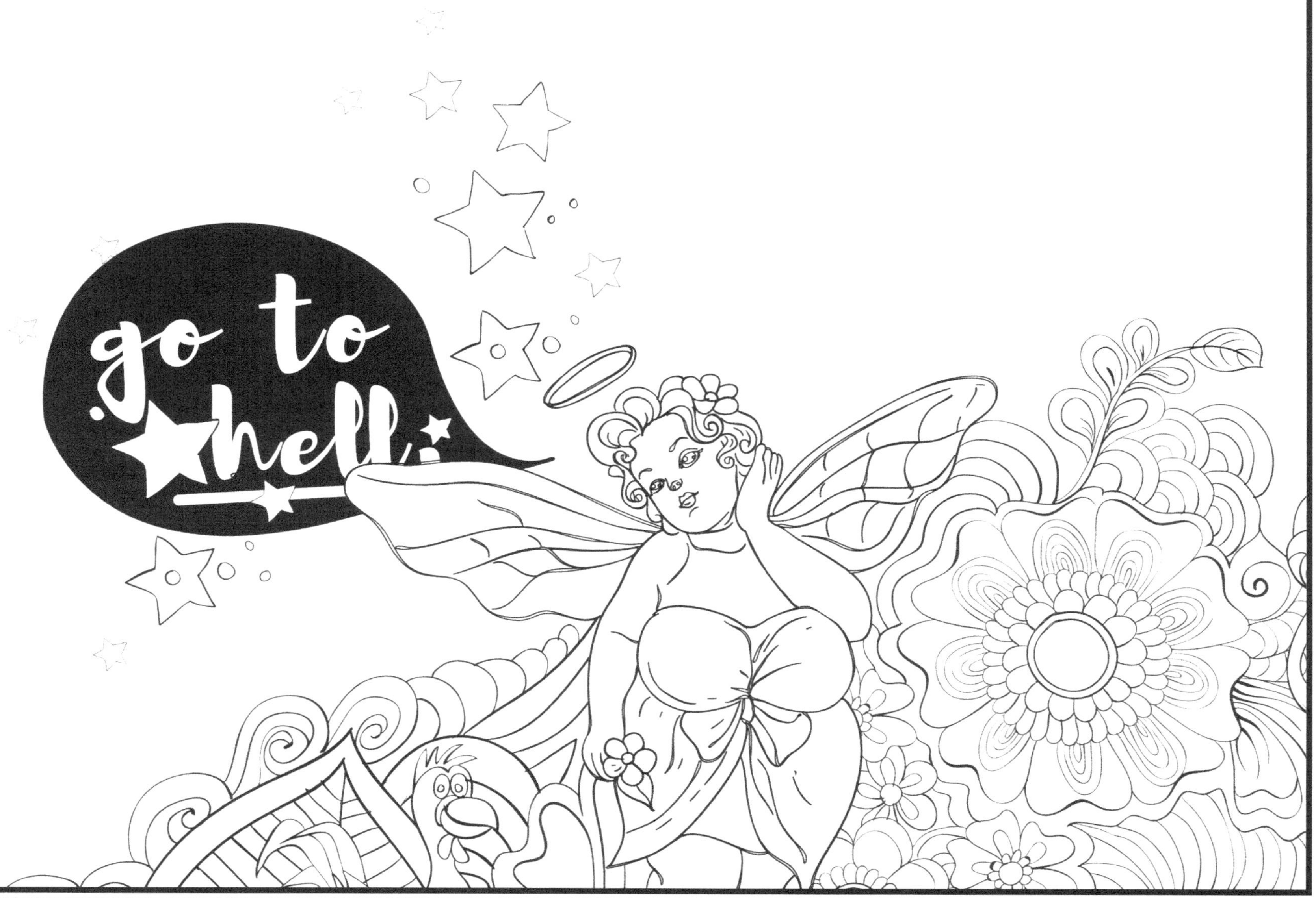
go to hell

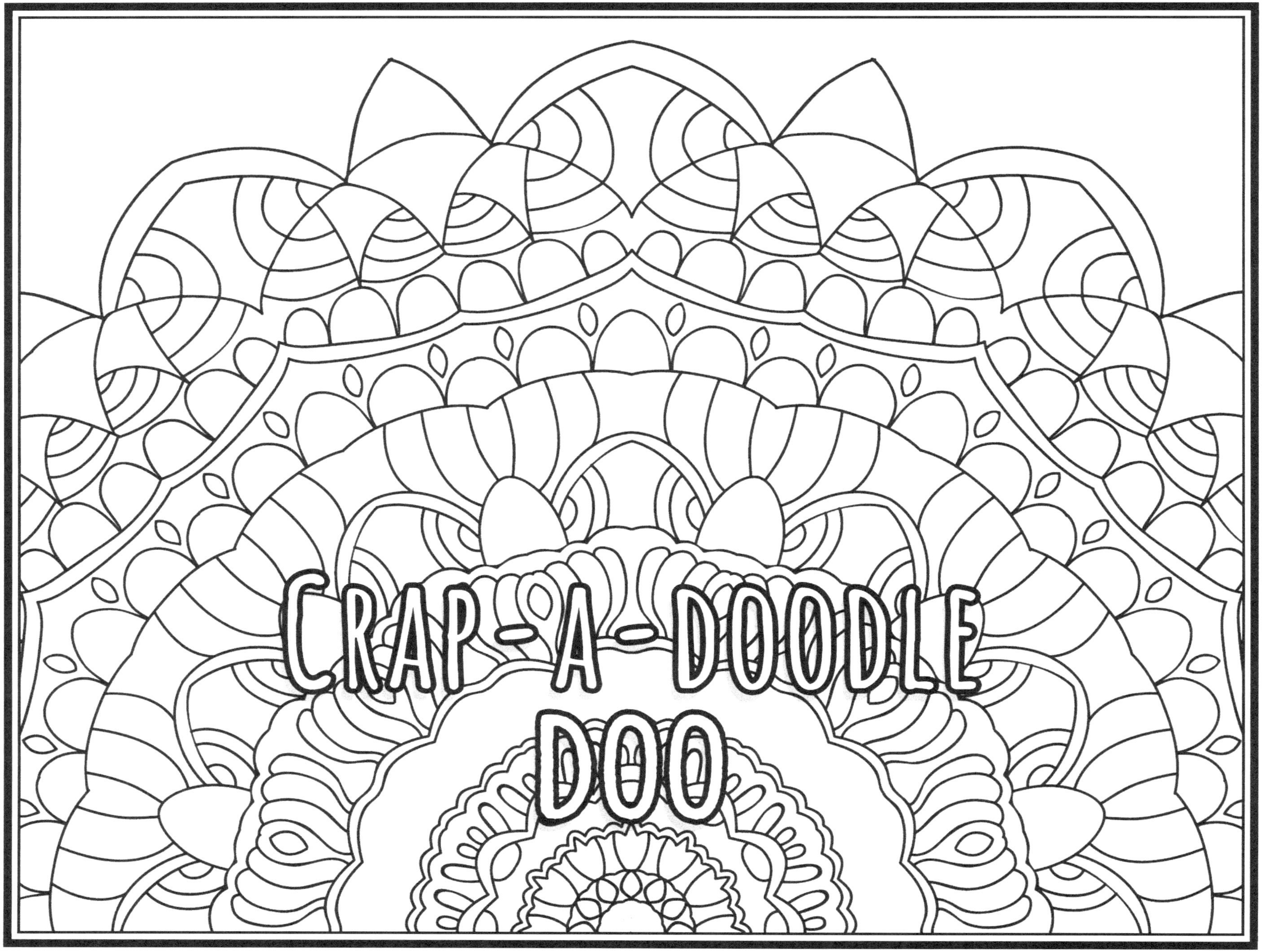
CRAP-A-DOODLE
DOO

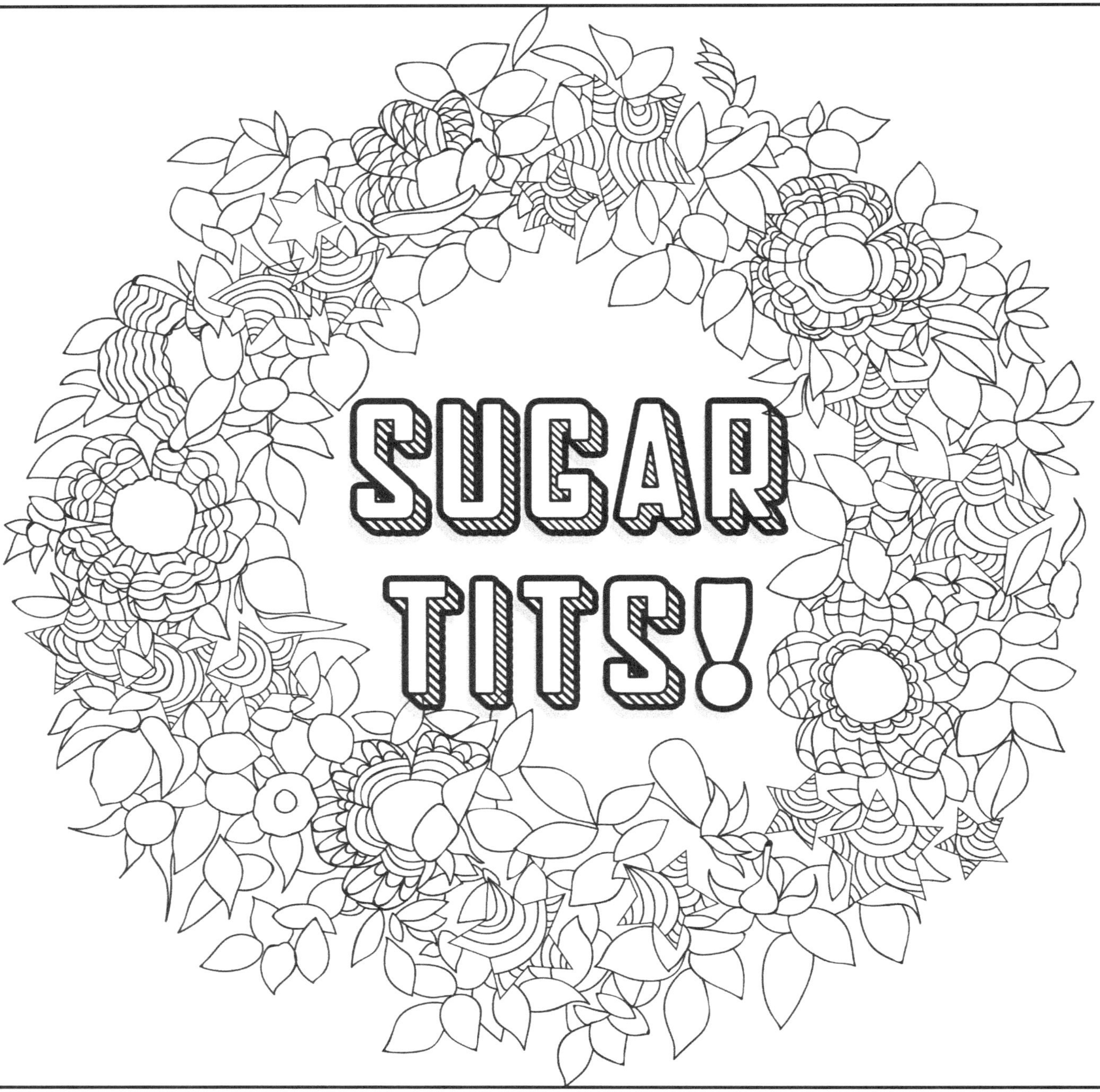
SUGAR
TITS!

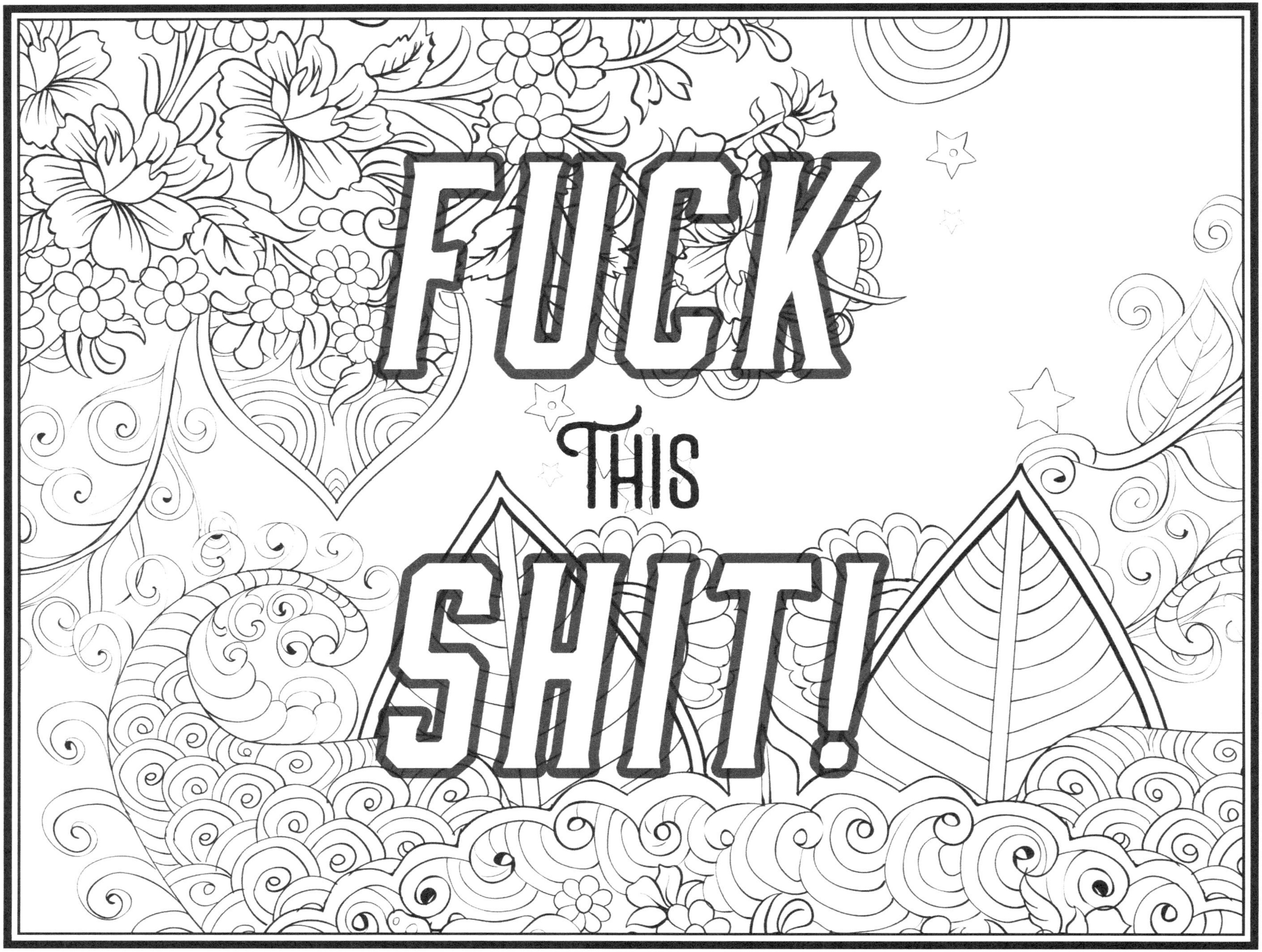
FUCK
THIS
SHIT!

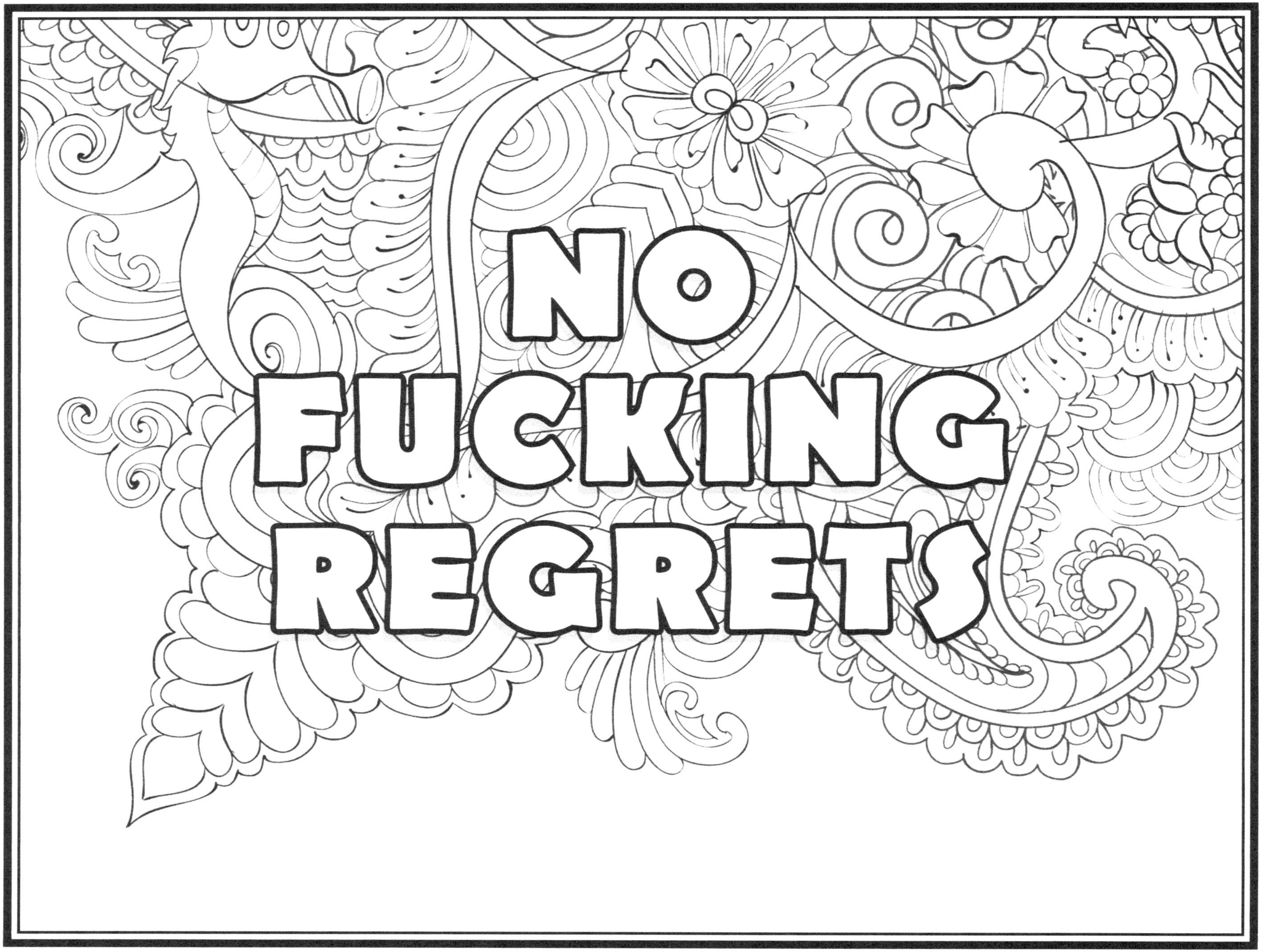
NO
FUCKING
REGRETS

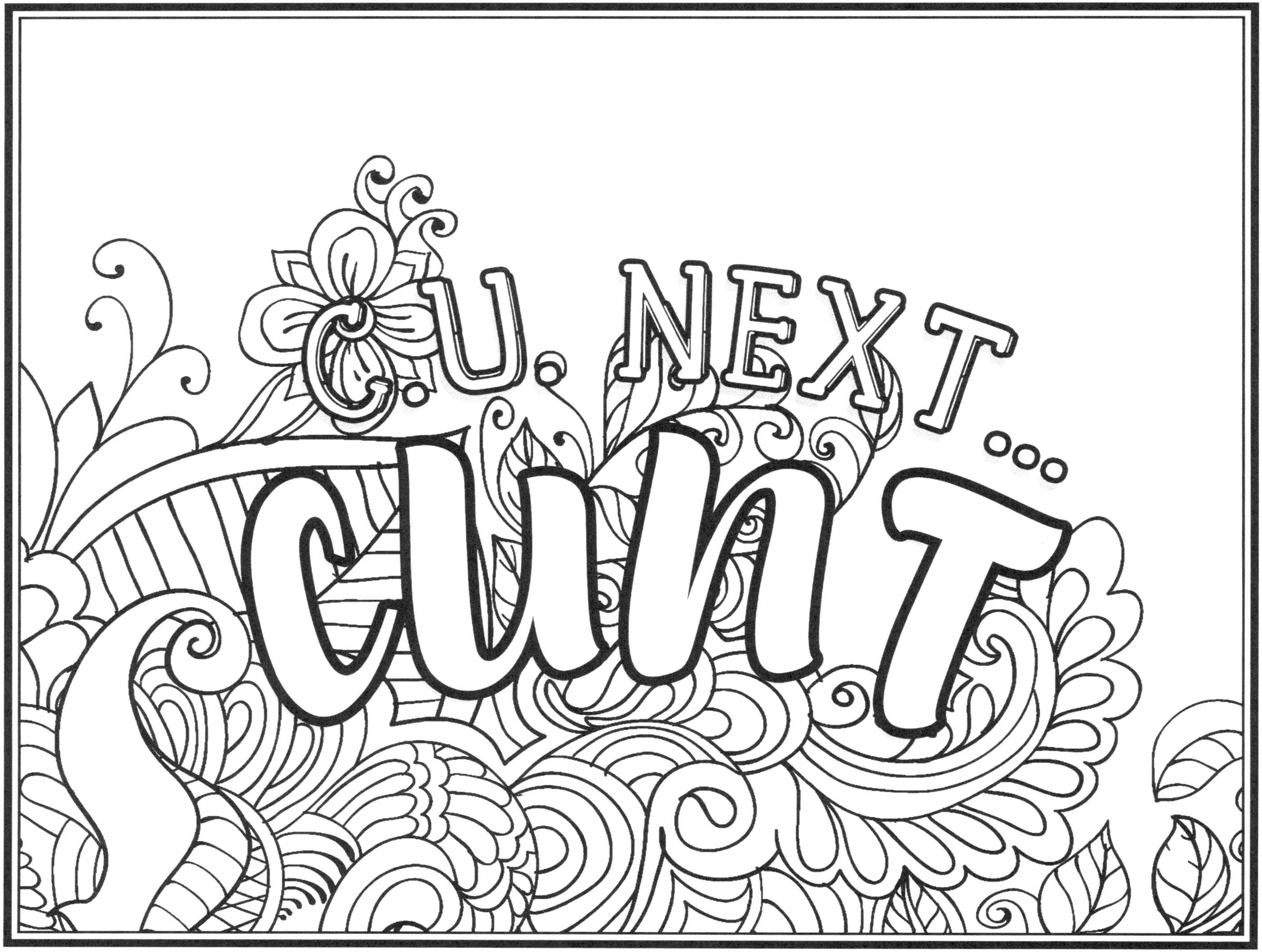
C.U. NEXT...
cunT

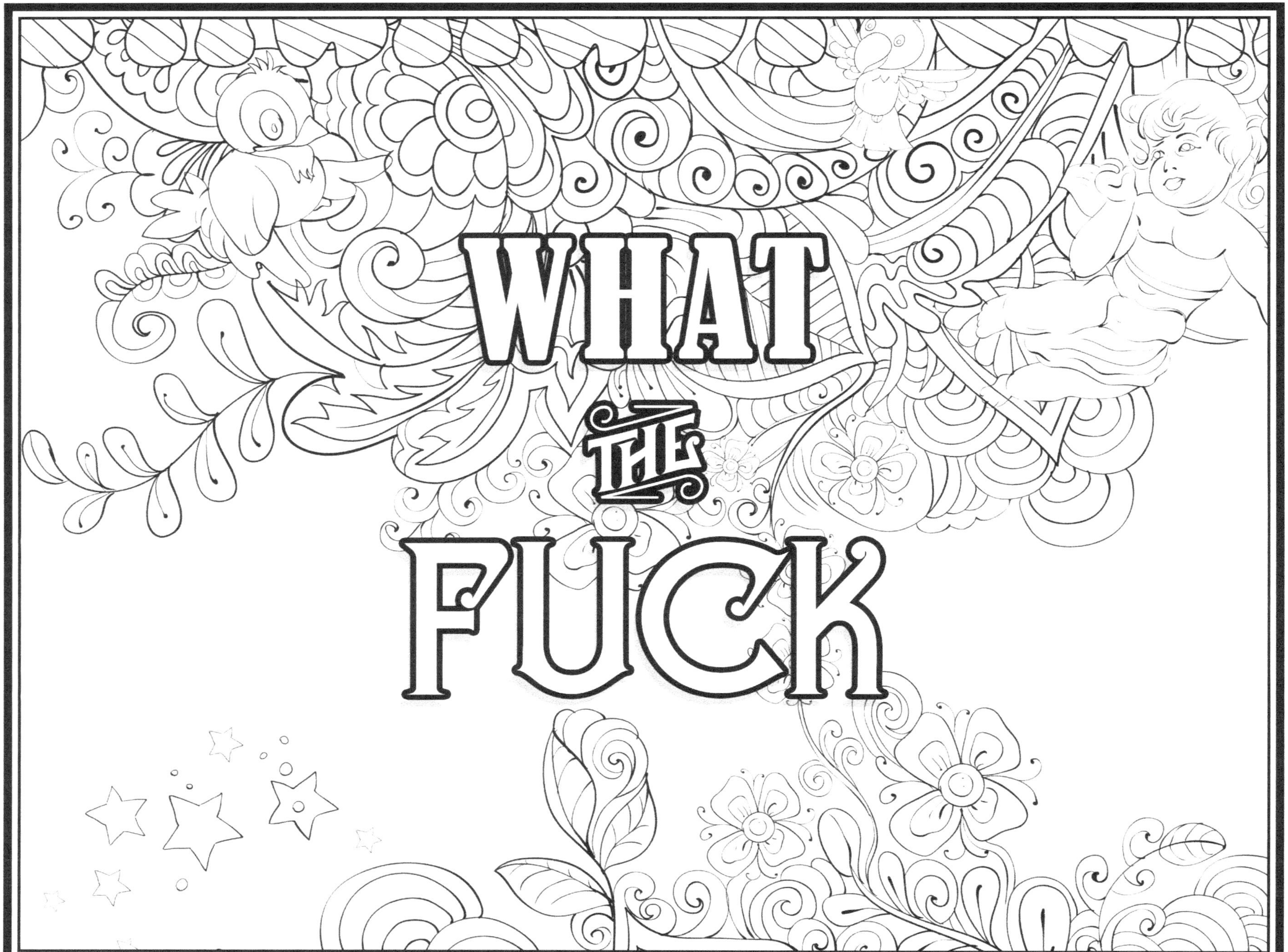
WHAT
THE
FUCK

www.ingramcontent.com/pod-product-compliance
Lightning Source LLC
Chambersburg PA
CBHW080643190526
45169CB00009B/3487
9781530142866